Table Of Contents

Chapter 1: The Hustle Begins	2
Chapter 2: Developing an Entrepreneurial Mindset	10
Chapter 3: Mastering Time Management	18
Chapter 4: Building Your Network	25
Chapter 5: Digital Marketing Essentials	33
Chapter 6: E-commerce Made Easy	41
Chapter 7: Achieving Work-Life Balance	48
Chapter 8: Staying Motivated and Resilient	56
Chapter 9: Developing Your Skills	64
Chapter 10: Your Path to Wealth	72

Chapter 1: The Hustle Begins

Embracing the Hustle Mentality

Embracing the hustle mentality is about igniting that inner fire and recognizing that your dreams are worth pursuing, no matter your current circumstances. For low-income earners and stay-at-home parents, this mindset isn't just beneficial; it's essential. It allows you to transform your passion into profit, leveraging your unique skills and experiences to create opportunities where none seemed to exist. Each small effort, every late-night brainstorming session, and every moment spent refining your craft contributes to building your empire from home. The hustle mentality empowers you to take control of your financial future and embrace the journey of entrepreneurship with zeal.

So let's start... Today you are going to build your "Hustle Muscle"!

At the core of the hustle mentality is the belief that hard work and persistence can lead to success. As aspiring entrepreneurs, you may encounter setbacks and challenges, but it is your resilience that will define your path. This is where time management techniques for side hustlers come into play. By prioritizing your tasks and setting clear goals, you can maximize your productivity without sacrificing family time or personal well-being. Remember, it's not about working harder; it's about working smarter. Embrace a schedule that allows you to maintain balance while striving for your dreams, and watch how your efforts start to compound.

Networking is another critical aspect of embracing the hustle mentality. It's not just about what you know; it's about who you know. Building relationships with like-minded individuals can provide you with invaluable support, insight, and opportunities. Attend local meetups, join online communities, or connect with other entrepreneurs on social media platforms. The connections you make can lead to partnerships, mentorships, and even potential clients for your side hustle. Each conversation is a stepping stone toward greater success, so don't shy away from reaching out and sharing your journey.

In today's digital age, understanding e-commerce strategies and digital marketing is crucial for any aspiring entrepreneur. Embracing the hustle means continuously learning and adapting to the ever-changing landscape of online business. Dive into resources, take courses, and experiment with different marketing techniques to find what resonates with your audience. Whether it's launching a small e-commerce store or promoting your freelance services, your willingness to learn and innovate will set you apart from the competition. Embrace the challenge, and remember that every successful entrepreneur started somewhere, often with just a single idea and a lot of determination.

Finally, embracing the hustle mentality also means recognizing the importance of motivation and work-life balance. Being driven is vital, but so is taking care of yourself and your loved ones. Make time for self-care, celebrate your small victories, and set realistic expectations. Understand that the road to success is a marathon, not a sprint. Cultivating resilience and maintaining your passion will keep you moving forward, even when the going gets tough. Surround yourself with positive influences, and remind yourself daily that your hustle is building not just an empire, but a legacy for you and your family. Together, with the right mindset and strategies, you can achieve your dreams and thrive in your entrepreneurial journey.

Setting Realistic Wealth Goals

Setting realistic wealth goals is a crucial step for anyone looking to build a financial future, especially for low-income earners and stay-at-home parents who are eager to create their own financial empires. The first step in this journey is to assess your current financial situation honestly. Take a deep breath and face your numbers head-on. Understanding your income, expenses, debts, and savings will provide a clear picture of where you stand. This evaluation is not just about crunching numbers; it's about recognizing your potential and setting the stage for your growth. Remember, every great empire starts with a solid foundation.

Once you have your financial picture, it's time to dream big but stay grounded. Wealth goals should inspire you, not intimidate you. Instead of saying, "I want to be a millionaire," think in terms of smaller, achievable milestones. For instance, aim to save a specific amount each month or to generate a certain income from your side hustle. These smaller, realistic goals can build your confidence and provide a sense of accomplishment along the way. Celebrate these victories! Each step forward is a building block toward your larger financial vision, and recognizing your progress can fuel your motivation.

As you set these goals, consider the time frame for each. Short-term goals can be those you aim to achieve within the next few months, such as creating a budget or starting a small online business. Medium-term goals might span a year or two, like saving enough for an emergency fund or investing in a skill development course. Long-term goals could involve planning for retirement or establishing a passive income stream. By breaking your goals into these time frames, you can maintain focus and adjust your strategies as needed. This approach ensures that you remain agile and open to new opportunities.

Networking is another essential component of setting realistic wealth goals. Surrounding yourself with like-minded individuals who share your aspirations can provide invaluable support and insights. Join community groups, online forums, or local meetups where you can connect with other aspiring entrepreneurs and side hustlers. Sharing your goals will not only keep you accountable but also open doors to new collaborations, resources, and opportunities you may not have considered. Remember, the journey to wealth is not a solitary one; the connections you make can significantly impact your success.

Lastly, embrace the mindset of resilience and adaptability. There will be challenges along the way, and that's perfectly okay. Stay committed to your goals, but be flexible in your approach. If something isn't working, reassess and pivot. The entrepreneurial journey is often filled with unexpected twists, so view each setback as a learning opportunity rather than a roadblock. By cultivating an enthusiastic and resilient attitude, you position yourself to turn obstacles into stepping stones, ultimately leading you closer to your wealth goals. Keep pushing forward; your empire is waiting to be built!

Crafting Your Personal Mission Statement

Crafting a personal mission statement is an empowering step in your journey toward wealth and fulfillment, especially for low-income earners, stay-at-home parents, and aspiring entrepreneurs. This statement acts as your compass, guiding your decisions and actions as you navigate the often challenging waters of building a business from home. It encapsulates your values, passions, and long-term goals, providing clarity and direction in your hustle. As you embark on this exciting journey, remember that your mission statement is unique to you and should reflect your individual aspirations.

To get started, take some time to reflect on what truly matters to you. Consider your core values and the reasons behind your desire to build wealth. Are you motivated by the desire to provide a better life for your family, or perhaps the dream of financial independence? Jot down your thoughts and feelings, allowing your passion to flow freely. This self-reflection will help you identify the key elements that should be included in your mission statement, ensuring it resonates with your personal journey and ambitions.

Next, think about the impact you want to make in your community and the lives of others. Your mission statement should not only serve your personal goals but also reflect how you wish to contribute positively to the world around you. Whether it's by inspiring fellow entrepreneurs, providing valuable resources, or creating job opportunities, consider how your unique journey can uplift others. By incorporating this aspect into your mission statement, you can create a sense of purpose that fuels your motivation and resilience as you hustle.

Once you have gathered your thoughts, it's time to craft your mission statement. Keep it concise and clear, focusing on the essence of what you stand for. A well-crafted mission statement should be easy to remember and serve as a daily reminder of your goals. For example, you might say, "I am dedicated to building a thriving online business that empowers my family and supports my community." Feel free to revise it as necessary; the beauty of a personal mission statement is that it evolves with you.

Finally, make it a habit to revisit and reflect on your mission statement regularly. As you grow and achieve new milestones, your goals may shift, and that's perfectly okay. Adjust your statement to align with your evolving aspirations and experiences, keeping it relevant and inspiring. By doing this, you will cultivate a strong entrepreneurial mindset that not only drives your hustle but also enhances your work-life balance. Remember, your mission statement is more than just words; it is a powerful tool that can transform your dreams into reality and guide you on the path to building your empire from home.

Chapter 2: Developing an Entrepreneurial Mindset

Cultivating a Growth Mindset

Cultivating a growth mindset is the key to unlocking your potential as a wealth builder, particularly when resources are limited. Embracing the belief that your abilities and intelligence can be developed through dedication and hard work is crucial. This mindset not only fosters a love for learning but also encourages resilience in the face of setbacks. As you embark on your journey to financial independence from home, remember that every obstacle is an opportunity to learn and grow. Your perspective can transform challenges into stepping stones toward your entrepreneurial goals.

To cultivate a growth mindset, start by reframing your thoughts around failure. Instead of viewing setbacks as a reflection of your abilities, see them as valuable lessons that contribute to your development. For instance, if a side hustle doesn't take off as expected, analyze what went wrong and apply those insights to your next venture. This approach not only builds your hustle muscle but also strengthens your entrepreneurial mindset, making you more adaptable and better equipped to seize future opportunities. Each experience, good or bad, adds to your toolkit for success.

Another essential aspect of nurturing a growth mindset is surrounding yourself with positivity and inspiration. Engage with like-minded individuals who share your passion for entrepreneurship, whether through online communities or local meetups. Networking with fellow hustlers helps you exchange ideas, gain insights, and cultivate a supportive environment. By immersing yourself in a community that values growth and learning, you'll find motivation and encouragement that propel you forward. Remember, the energy of those around you can significantly influence your mindset and ambition.

Time management is a crucial skill for anyone balancing multiple responsibilities, especially stay-at-home parents and low-income earners. Prioritizing tasks and setting realistic goals can help you maximize your productivity while nurturing a growth mindset. Break down your objectives into manageable steps, and celebrate small victories along the way. This approach not only keeps you motivated but also reinforces the belief that consistent effort leads to progress. As you recognize your accomplishments, no matter how minor, you'll cultivate a sense of confidence that fuels your entrepreneurial journey.

Finally, never underestimate the power of self-reflection and continuous learning. Set aside time to assess your growth, identify areas for improvement, and seek out new skills relevant to your entrepreneurial ambitions. Whether through online courses, podcasts, or books, investing in your personal development is essential. Embrace the idea that becoming a successful entrepreneur is a marathon, not a sprint. With each step you take and every skill you acquire, you're not just building a financial empire; you're also fostering a mindset that thrives on challenge, resilience, and lifelong learning. Embrace this journey, and watch how your growth mindset transforms your aspirations into reality.

Overcoming Fear of Failure

Fear of failure can be a significant barrier for many aspiring entrepreneurs, especially for those on a tight budget. However, embracing this fear is crucial for anyone looking to build their wealth from home. Instead of letting fear paralyze you, consider it a natural part of the entrepreneurial journey. The most successful entrepreneurs have faced setbacks; what distinguishes them is their willingness to learn from these experiences. By reframing your perception of failure, you can transform it from a stumbling block into a stepping stone towards your goals.

One effective way to overcome the fear of failure is to adopt a growth mindset. This means viewing challenges as opportunities for growth rather than threats to your self-worth. When you approach your side hustle with the understanding that mistakes are part of the learning process, you will find it easier to take risks. This mindset encourages experimentation, which is vital for building hustle muscle. Each attempt, whether successful or not, contributes to your knowledge and skill set, making you a more resilient entrepreneur.

Networking is another powerful tool in overcoming fear of failure. Surrounding yourself with like-minded individuals who share your entrepreneurial aspirations can provide the support you need to take bold steps. Joining local business groups, attending workshops, or participating in online forums can help you connect with others who have faced similar fears. These connections often lead to valuable mentorship opportunities, collaboration, and encouragement. Remember, every successful entrepreneur has once stood where you are now, feeling uncertain and afraid.

Time management techniques can also play a pivotal role in conquering fear of failure. By organizing your tasks and breaking your goals into manageable steps, you can reduce anxiety and increase your confidence. Setting small, achievable milestones allows you to celebrate your progress, helping you build a sense of accomplishment. This incremental approach not only makes your goals feel more attainable but also reinforces a positive mindset, enabling you to tackle larger challenges without the overwhelming fear of failure looming over you.

Finally, cultivating motivation and resilience is essential in your journey to overcome fear. Embrace your passion and remind yourself of your 'why'—the reason you started your entrepreneurial journey. Create a vision board or journal your goals to keep your aspirations front and center. When setbacks occur, which they inevitably will, draw on your inner strength and the support of your network. Understand that every failure is an opportunity for growth, and with each obstacle you overcome, you solidify your path toward building your empire from home.

Visualization Techniques for Success

Visualization techniques are powerful tools that can help you turn your dreams into reality, especially when you're working within a limited budget. For low-income earners and stay-at-home parents, visualizing your goals can provide clarity and motivation. Imagine crafting a vivid mental picture of your ideal life, where your side hustle flourishes, your entrepreneurial spirit shines, and you achieve the financial freedom you aspire to. By creating a clear vision, you set the stage for success, allowing your mind to work towards making that vision a tangible part of your everyday life.

One effective visualization technique is the creation of a vision board. Gather images, quotes, and symbols that represent your goals and desires. This could include pictures of your dream home, inspiring entrepreneurs you admire, or representations of the skills you want to develop. Place your vision board in a prominent spot where you see it daily. This constant reminder will keep your goals at the forefront of your mind, motivating you to take the necessary steps to realize them. Each time you glance at your board, you reinforce your commitment to building your empire from home.

Another valuable technique is guided visualization, which involves relaxing your mind and picturing yourself achieving specific goals. Find a quiet space, close your eyes, and take deep breaths. Imagine yourself successfully launching your e-commerce site or mastering digital marketing strategies. Feel the emotions associated with that success—pride, excitement, and fulfillment. This practice not only boosts your motivation but also enhances your confidence, enabling you to approach challenges with a resilient mindset that is essential for any aspiring entrepreneur.

Incorporating visualization into your daily routine can significantly enhance your time management techniques. Start each day by spending a few minutes visualizing your schedule and the tasks you need to accomplish. Picture yourself efficiently managing your time, balancing family responsibilities, and dedicating focused hours to your side hustle. By mentally rehearsing your day, you can build a clearer roadmap and anticipate potential obstacles, making it easier to navigate your responsibilities without feeling overwhelmed.

Finally, don't underestimate the power of visualization when it comes to networking strategies. Envision yourself engaging with successful entrepreneurs and potential collaborators. Picture the conversations you want to have, the connections you want to forge, and the opportunities that will arise from those interactions. This mental exercise can help you approach networking with confidence, allowing you to step out of your comfort zone and build meaningful relationships that will support your entrepreneurial journey. With these visualization techniques in your toolkit, you are well on your way to building your wealth and achieving your dreams, all from the comfort of your home.

Chapter 3: Mastering Time Management

Identifying Your Most Productive Hours

Identifying your most productive hours is a game changer for anyone looking to maximize their output without sacrificing personal time. As low-income earners and aspiring entrepreneurs, it's essential to leverage every minute effectively. You might be juggling multiple responsibilities—whether it's caring for children, working a day job, or managing a side hustle. The key lies in understanding when you are naturally inclined to be at your best. This process involves self-reflection and experimentation, so grab a notebook and start tracking your energy levels throughout the day.

Begin by taking note of your daily routines for at least a week. Document when you feel most alert and focused, as well as when you hit those inevitable energy slumps. For some, the early morning hours before the world wakes up can be a golden time for creativity and productivity, while others may find their stride in the late evening. Recognizing these patterns will allow you to carve out specific time blocks dedicated to your most important tasks. Harnessing these peak hours means you can achieve more in less time, whether you're brainstorming your next business idea or working on your e-commerce store.

Once you've identified these productive windows, it's time to align your most critical tasks with them. Prioritize your side hustle strategies, skill development, or networking during these high-energy periods. If you're a stay-at-home parent, this might mean setting aside time when the kids are napping or after they've gone to bed. By optimizing your schedule around your natural rhythms, you'll find that work feels less like a chore and more like an exciting adventure. You'll be amazed at how much more you can accomplish when you're working during your peak hours.

Additionally, don't be afraid to adjust your environment to enhance your productivity. Find a space that inspires you, whether it's a cozy corner of your home or a local café. Minimize distractions by setting boundaries with family or using tools like noise-canceling headphones. The right environment, combined with your identified productive hours, can create a powerful synergy that propels you toward your goals. Remember, it's not just about working harder; it's about working smarter.

Lastly, be patient and flexible with yourself as you refine this process. Life can be unpredictable, especially for those balancing multiple roles. Track your progress and adjust your schedule as needed. Celebrate small wins and stay motivated by recognizing how far you've come. Each step you take toward understanding and utilizing your most productive hours will bring you closer to building your empire from home. Embrace the journey, and let your newfound insights fuel your entrepreneurial spirit!

The Art of Prioritization

In the journey of building wealth on a budget, mastering the art of prioritization can be your secret weapon. For low-income earners and stay-at-home parents alike, the challenge often lies in juggling multiple responsibilities while striving to create a thriving side hustle. By identifying your priorities, you not only streamline your efforts but also maximize the impact of your time and resources. Start by distinguishing what is urgent from what is important; this clear delineation will empower you to focus on activities that propel your entrepreneurial dreams forward.

As you navigate the world of wealth-building, it's crucial to harness the power of the entrepreneurial mindset. This mindset thrives on resilience and adaptability, allowing you to pivot when necessary. Make a list of your goals and categorize them based on their potential return on investment—both in terms of time and finances. Prioritization isn't just about ticking off tasks on a to-do list; it's about aligning your efforts with your ultimate vision. This strategic approach will enable you to allocate your resources effectively, ensuring that your energy is focused on tasks that yield the greatest results.

Time management techniques are essential for side hustlers, particularly those balancing family commitments. Implementing methods like the Eisenhower Box can revolutionize how you approach daily tasks. By dividing your tasks into four categories—urgent and important, important but not urgent, urgent but not important, and neither urgent nor important—you can make informed decisions about where to invest your time. This clarity will help you sidestep burnout and maintain enthusiasm for your entrepreneurial pursuits, all while managing household responsibilities.

Networking is another vital aspect of prioritization. As aspiring entrepreneurs, building connections can open doors that lead to collaboration, mentorship, and new opportunities. Prioritize attending local networking events or engaging in online communities where you can share experiences and gain insights from others on similar journeys. By fostering relationships with individuals who share your goals, you create a supportive environment that motivates you to stay focused and committed to your wealth-building strategies.

Finally, don't underestimate the importance of work-life balance. As you prioritize tasks, remember to carve out time for self-care and family. Building an empire from home is a marathon, not a sprint. By recognizing the value of rest and rejuvenation, you can sustain your motivation and resilience over the long haul. Balancing your entrepreneurial endeavors with personal fulfillment will not only enhance your productivity but also create a fulfilling life that reflects your values and aspirations. Embrace the art of prioritization, and watch how it transforms your journey towards building wealth on a budget.

Creating a Daily Schedule That Works

Creating a daily schedule that works is the cornerstone of turning your dreams into reality, especially when you're building wealth on a budget. For low-income earners, stay-at-home parents, and aspiring entrepreneurs, a well-structured day can be your secret weapon. Think of your schedule as a roadmap that guides you through the hustle and bustle of life. It's not just about filling the hours; it's about maximizing your productivity so you can carve out time for your side hustles, skill development, and networking opportunities. With a bit of enthusiasm and commitment, you can create a daily routine that fuels your entrepreneurial spirit.

Start by identifying your priorities. What are the key tasks that will move you closer to your goals? Whether it's developing your e-commerce strategy, honing your digital marketing skills, or networking with fellow hustlers, understanding what truly matters is crucial. Dedicate specific time slots for these activities in your daily schedule. By making them non-negotiable, you create a sense of accountability. Remember, consistency is key. The more you stick to your schedule, the more progress you'll see, and the more motivated you'll feel to keep pushing forward.

Next, embrace the power of time blocking. This technique involves dividing your day into distinct blocks of time, each dedicated to a specific activity. For instance, reserve the early morning hours for focused work on your side hustle while the kids are still asleep. Use the late afternoon for skill development, perhaps through online courses or webinars. By compartmentalizing your time, you can minimize distractions and increase your efficiency. This approach not only helps you stay organized but also allows you to balance your responsibilities as a parent and entrepreneur.

Don't forget to build in breaks and self-care into your schedule. Maintaining a healthy work-life balance is essential for long-term success and resilience. Schedule short breaks to recharge, whether that's taking a walk, enjoying a cup of tea, or engaging in a quick mindfulness exercise. By nurturing your mental and physical well-being, you'll be better equipped to tackle challenges and remain motivated. Remember, entrepreneurship is a marathon, not a sprint, and taking care of yourself is crucial for sustaining your hustle.

Finally, be adaptable. Life is unpredictable, especially when juggling family responsibilities and entrepreneurial pursuits. Don't be afraid to tweak your schedule as needed. If something isn't working, reassess and make adjustments. Flexibility is a vital skill for any entrepreneur, and being open to change will help you navigate the ups and downs of your journey. Celebrate your small victories along the way, and stay enthusiastic about your progress. With a daily schedule that works, you're not just building wealth; you're building a fulfilling life that aligns with your dreams and aspirations.

Chapter 4: Building Your Network

Finding Your Tribe

Finding your tribe is an essential step in building your empire from home, especially when you're navigating the challenges of low income and limited resources. Surrounding yourself with like-minded individuals who share your goals and aspirations can propel you forward in your journey to wealth. These connections can inspire you, provide valuable insights, and keep you motivated when the going gets tough. Whether you're a stay-at-home parent or an aspiring entrepreneur, finding a supportive community can make all the difference.

Start by exploring local meetups, online forums, and social media groups tailored to your interests. Look for platforms that cater specifically to your niche, such as entrepreneurial mindset development or digital marketing for startups. Engaging with others who are on similar paths can help you exchange ideas, troubleshoot challenges, and celebrate each other's successes. Remember, every connection you make could lead to new opportunities, collaborations, or even friendships that enrich your journey.

Networking isn't just about exchanging business cards; it's about building genuine relationships. When you find your tribe, invest time in nurturing these connections. Attend events, participate in discussions, and be proactive in offering help to others. By being a resource for your peers, you'll not only strengthen your network but also position yourself as a valuable member of your community. This reciprocity fosters an environment of support, where everyone is invested in each other's growth.

Embrace the power of digital tools to expand your tribe beyond geographical limitations. Online platforms allow you to connect with entrepreneurs and wealth builders from all over the world. Use social media to follow and engage with influencers in your niche, join relevant Facebook groups, or participate in webinars and online courses. These virtual communities can provide fresh perspectives and innovative strategies that can elevate your hustle muscle and entrepreneurial mindset.

Finally, remember that finding your tribe is an ongoing journey. As you evolve and grow, your network should too. Stay open to meeting new people, learning from diverse experiences, and adapting to changes in your goals. The right tribe can provide not just motivation and resilience, but also accountability, encouragement, and a sense of belonging. Together, you can conquer challenges, celebrate milestones, and build an empire—all from the comfort of your home!

Leveraging Social Media for Connections

In today's digital age, social media has transformed the way we connect, making it an invaluable tool for low-income earners and aspiring entrepreneurs. Leveraging social media effectively can open doors to opportunities that were once out of reach, allowing you to network with like-minded individuals, potential clients, and mentors. Imagine being able to tap into a global community of entrepreneurs who share your passion for building wealth while navigating the challenges of life on a budget. This is not just a dream; it's a reality waiting for you to seize!

Building your brand on social media platforms can significantly enhance your entrepreneurial journey. By consistently sharing your insights, successes, and even your struggles, you position yourself as an authentic voice in your niche. This transparency fosters trust and attracts followers who resonate with your story. When you create valuable content, whether it's tips on time management or motivation for fellow hustlers, you not only help others but also establish yourself as an authority in your field. Remember, every post is an opportunity to showcase your expertise and passion, drawing people toward your unique vision.

Networking on social media goes beyond merely accumulating followers; it's about cultivating genuine relationships. Engage with your audience by responding to comments, participating in discussions, and collaborating with others in your niche. Find groups on platforms like Facebook or LinkedIn that cater to your interests, and actively contribute to conversations. By doing so, you'll discover potential partners, clients, or mentors who can provide invaluable guidance on your journey. Each connection you make can lead to new opportunities, so don't underestimate the power of a simple comment or message.

Moreover, social media can be a powerful marketing tool for your side hustle or startup. Utilize platforms like Instagram and TikTok to showcase your products or services creatively. Share behind-the-scenes content that highlights your process, and use engaging visuals to attract attention. Remember, storytelling is key; your audience wants to connect with the person behind the brand. By sharing your journey, you not only promote your offerings but also inspire others to take action. The right social media strategy can create a ripple effect, attracting customers and expanding your reach without breaking the bank.

Finally, maintaining a healthy work-life balance while navigating the demands of entrepreneurship is crucial. Social media allows you to schedule posts and automate certain tasks, freeing up your time for family and self-care. Set boundaries for your online presence; remember that it's okay to unplug and focus on what truly matters. By prioritizing your well-being, you'll be more resilient in the face of challenges. Leverage social media to connect, inspire, and grow, but always keep your personal goals and values at the forefront. Your journey is uniquely yours – embrace it with enthusiasm, and watch your empire flourish!

Networking Events and Online Communities

Networking events and online communities are powerful tools for low-income earners and aspiring entrepreneurs looking to build their wealth from home. These platforms provide invaluable opportunities to connect with like-minded individuals, gain insights into various industries, and share experiences that can elevate your entrepreneurial journey. Whether you're a stay-at-home parent seeking flexible income or someone trying to find your hustle muscle, the right connections can make all the difference. By engaging in these environments, you can discover resources, mentorship, and partnerships that can propel your side hustle forward.

Attending networking events, even if virtually, allows you to meet others who are on similar paths. These gatherings often feature workshops, panel discussions, and keynote speeches from seasoned entrepreneurs who have navigated the challenges you face. Don't underestimate the power of a simple conversation. Sharing your story and listening to others can spark ideas and motivate you to take action. Plus, networking events often provide access to potential clients, collaborators, and even investors who believe in supporting budding entrepreneurs. The more you immerse yourself in these environments, the more opportunities you create for yourself.

Online communities have revolutionized how we connect and collaborate. Platforms like Facebook groups, LinkedIn, and specialized forums offer spaces tailored for aspiring entrepreneurs. Here, you can seek advice, share resources, and exchange feedback on your projects. The beauty of these communities is that they often consist of individuals from diverse backgrounds, each bringing unique perspectives and skills to the table. Joining discussions or starting your own can help you find your voice and establish your presence in your niche. Remember, your insights might inspire someone else on their journey!

As you navigate these networking avenues, focus on building genuine relationships rather than just collecting contacts. This approach fosters trust and encourages collaboration, which is essential for long-term success. Share your knowledge, ask questions, and be open to learning from others. Many successful entrepreneurs attribute their growth to the strong connections they've formed over time. By being proactive, you can create a supportive network that not only motivates you but also holds you accountable in your wealth-building journey.

Lastly, don't forget to leverage digital marketing strategies to extend your reach within these communities. Share your experiences, promote your side hustle, and engage with others through content creation. Whether it's through blog posts, social media updates, or videos, showcasing your journey can attract the right audience and collaborators. Remember, every interaction is an opportunity to learn and grow. Embrace the enthusiasm of connecting with others, and watch your empire flourish from the comfort of your home!

Chapter 5: Digital Marketing Essentials

Understanding Your Target Audience

Understanding your target audience is the cornerstone of building a successful venture, especially for low-income earners and aspiring entrepreneurs. When you take the time to truly understand who you are serving, you unlock the door to creating products and services that resonate deeply with them. For stay-at-home parents, wealth builders, and those working tirelessly to elevate their financial status, knowing their needs, preferences, and pain points can set you apart from the crowd. You're not just selling a product; you're providing a solution that addresses their specific challenges and aspirations.

To connect with your audience effectively, start by defining who they are. Consider their demographics, interests, and lifestyles. For example, many stay-at-home parents may be juggling multiple responsibilities while aspiring to create a side hustle. They might crave flexibility and tools that help them manage their time efficiently. Understanding these aspects allows you to tailor your messaging and offerings in a way that speaks directly to their circumstances. When your audience feels understood and valued, they're more likely to engage and invest in what you have to offer.

Next, dive into the psychology of your target audience. What motivates them? What hurdles do they face in their journey toward financial independence? For individuals building their "hustle muscle," it's essential to recognize that motivation can fluctuate. Some days are filled with inspiration, while others may feel overwhelming. By tapping into their emotional landscape, you can create content that inspires resilience and keeps them moving forward. Whether it's through motivational stories, practical tips on time management, or powerful networking strategies, your goal is to empower them to keep pushing toward their goals.

Don't overlook the importance of feedback and interaction. Engaging with your audience not only helps you refine your understanding of their needs but also builds a community around your brand. Utilize social media platforms, surveys, and forums to gain insights directly from those you aim to serve. Listen actively to their struggles and triumphs, and be willing to adapt your approach based on their input. This two-way communication fosters trust and loyalty, which are invaluable assets in any entrepreneurial journey.

Finally, remember that your target audience is dynamic. As they grow and evolve, so too will their needs and desires. Stay informed about trends in the entrepreneurial landscape, digital marketing strategies, and the latest techniques in e-commerce. Continuously educating yourself will enable you to serve your audience better and remain relevant in a fast-paced world. By committing to understanding your audience deeply and adapting to their changing landscape, you position yourself as a trusted ally in their pursuit of wealth and fulfillment. Together, you can build an empire from home, one step at a time!

Building a Strong Online Presence

Building a strong online presence is essential for anyone looking to thrive in today's digital world, especially for low-income earners and aspiring entrepreneurs. The internet provides a vast landscape filled with opportunities where you can showcase your skills, connect with like-minded individuals, and attract potential clients. Whether you're a stay-at-home parent with a side hustle or someone who dreams of building a business empire from home, understanding how to effectively leverage online platforms can dramatically accelerate your journey toward financial freedom.

First, start by establishing your personal brand. This doesn't require a massive budget; instead, focus on authenticity and clarity. Share your story, your passions, and what sets you apart. Create profiles on social media platforms that resonate with your target audience, such as Instagram, LinkedIn, or Facebook. Consistency is key—use the same profile picture and bio across platforms to create a cohesive identity. As you share your journey, engage with your audience by asking questions, responding to comments, and fostering a community. This connection will not only build trust but will also establish you as an authority in your niche.

Next, invest time in learning digital marketing strategies that can amplify your online presence. You don't need to be a tech wizard; numerous free resources and tutorials are available to help you understand the basics of SEO, content marketing, and social media advertising. Start by creating valuable content that addresses the needs and pain points of your audience. Whether it's blog posts, videos, or podcasts, showcasing your expertise will attract people to your brand. Remember, the goal is to provide value—when people find your content helpful, they are more likely to share it, expanding your reach without additional costs.

Networking is another powerful tool for building your online presence. Connect with other entrepreneurs, influencers, and potential clients in your niche. Attend virtual workshops, join online forums, and participate in social media groups. These platforms are gold mines for building relationships and gathering insights that can propel your hustle forward. Collaborate with others on projects or co-host events; this not only broadens your audience but also enriches your experience as you learn from others' expertise and perspectives.

Finally, maintain a healthy work-life balance as you cultivate your online presence. It's easy to get caught up in the hustle and lose sight of what really matters. Set boundaries for your online activities, allocate specific times for social media engagement, and remember to take breaks. Use tools and apps to manage your time effectively, allowing you to focus on building your business while still enjoying precious moments with family and friends. Embrace the journey with enthusiasm and resilience, knowing that every effort you put into building a strong online presence is a step closer to your financial goals.

Cost-Effective Marketing Strategies

Cost-effective marketing strategies are essential for anyone looking to build their empire from home, especially if you're navigating the challenges of a limited budget. In today's digital age, there are countless tools and platforms available that can help you promote your business without breaking the bank. One of the most effective approaches is leveraging social media. Platforms like Facebook, Instagram, and Twitter offer incredible opportunities for organic reach. Engage with your audience through authentic posts, stories, and live sessions, showcasing your journey and the value of your products or services. This not only builds a loyal community but also fosters connections that can lead to word-of-mouth referrals.

Content marketing is another powerful strategy that can yield significant returns without a hefty investment. Start a blog or a YouTube channel to share valuable insights related to your niche. Whether it's tips on time management, entrepreneurial mindset development, or ways to maintain work-life balance, providing useful content positions you as an authority in your field. Consistently creating high-quality content not only attracts potential customers but also helps with search engine optimization (SEO), making it easier for people to find you online. Plus, the more you share your knowledge, the more you'll inspire others and build your brand's credibility.

Networking, often overlooked, can be one of the most cost-effective marketing strategies for aspiring entrepreneurs. Attend local meetups, workshops, or online webinars relevant to your niche. Building relationships with fellow entrepreneurs can lead to collaborations, referrals, and invaluable advice. Don't underestimate the power of word-of-mouth; personal recommendations can bring in clients who are eager to work with you based on trust. Moreover, consider joining online entrepreneurial communities and forums where you can connect with like-minded individuals, share experiences, and promote each other's work.

Email marketing is a fantastic way to reach your audience directly without incurring significant costs. Start by building an email list through sign-ups on your website or social media platforms. Offer a free resource, like an e-book or checklist related to skill development for freelancers, as an incentive for subscriptions. Once you have a list, craft engaging newsletters with updates, valuable tips, and special offers. Regular communication keeps your audience engaged and informed, increasing the likelihood of converting subscribers into loyal customers.

Lastly, consider utilizing free or low-cost tools to streamline your marketing efforts. Platforms like Canva allow you to create stunning graphics for social media, while Hootsuite or Buffer can help you schedule posts in advance, saving you time and ensuring consistency. Explore free trials of various tools to find what best fits your needs, and don't shy away from DIY solutions. With a little creativity and a strategic mindset, you can effectively market your business, build connections, and grow your empire—all while staying within your budget. Embrace these cost-effective strategies and watch your entrepreneurial dreams take flight!

Chapter 6: E-commerce Made Easy

Choosing the Right Platform

Choosing the right platform is a crucial step in your journey to building wealth on a budget. With a myriad of options available, from social media channels to e-commerce sites and freelancing platforms, it can be overwhelming to determine which avenue aligns best with your goals and skills. As low-income earners and stay-at-home parents, it's essential to choose a platform that not only fits your current resources but also maximizes your potential for growth. Remember, the right platform can serve as the launchpad for your entrepreneurial dreams, paving the way for success.

When considering your options, think about your strengths and interests. Are you an excellent communicator with a knack for storytelling? Platforms like Instagram or TikTok may be ideal for you to showcase your creativity and connect with an audience. Alternatively, if you have a talent for crafting or coding, e-commerce platforms like Etsy or Shopify could provide the perfect marketplace for your products. By aligning your chosen platform with your passions and skills, you set yourself up for a fulfilling journey that keeps you motivated and engaged.

Time management is another crucial factor in selecting the right platform. As busy hustlers, you need a platform that allows you to work efficiently while balancing family and personal commitments. Consider platforms that offer user-friendly interfaces and streamlined processes. For instance, if you're diving into digital marketing, tools like Mailchimp or Canva can simplify your efforts, saving you precious hours. Choose platforms that enable you to automate tasks, allowing you to focus on what truly matters: building your brand and connecting with your audience.

Networking strategies play a significant role in your success, and the platform you choose can greatly influence your ability to connect with others. Look for platforms that foster community engagement, such as Facebook groups or LinkedIn. These spaces can be invaluable for sharing experiences, learning from fellow entrepreneurs, and even finding mentorship opportunities. The right platform will not only help you establish your presence but also connect you with like-minded individuals who can support your journey and inspire you to keep pushing forward.

Lastly, don't underestimate the importance of motivation and resilience in your entrepreneurial endeavors. The platform you choose should inspire you to keep learning and growing, even when challenges arise. Seek out spaces that offer educational resources, workshops, and forums where you can gain insights from others' experiences. Embrace platforms that encourage continuous skill development, so you can adapt and thrive in an ever-changing landscape. With the right platform, you'll find not just a means to an end, but a vibrant community that fuels your ambition and supports your dreams of building wealth on a budget.

Sourcing Products on a Budget

Sourcing products on a budget can be a game changer for low-income earners and aspiring entrepreneurs. When you're building your empire from home, every dollar counts, and finding the right products at the right price can lay the foundation for your success. Whether you're a stay-at-home parent looking to bring in extra income or a hustler trying to make your mark, mastering the art of budget-friendly sourcing will empower you to create a thriving business without breaking the bank.

Start by tapping into your local community for resources. Thrift stores, garage sales, and flea markets are treasure troves for unique products that can be resold at a profit. Not only will you save money, but you'll also discover items that are one-of-a-kind, giving your business a distinct edge. Networking with fellow entrepreneurs in your area can lead to collaborative opportunities where you share sourcing tips and even bulk purchase items together, further reducing costs. Remember, every connection you make is a step toward building your hustle muscle.

Online platforms also offer incredible opportunities for budget-conscious entrepreneurs. Websites like Alibaba, Etsy, and even eBay can connect you with wholesalers and artisans from around the globe. By leveraging these platforms, you can find products that align with your vision without emptying your pockets. Don't forget to explore dropshipping as a strategy—this way, you can sell products without holding any inventory, which minimizes upfront costs and risks. With a little research, you can discover suppliers who offer quality products at competitive prices.

Utilizing digital marketing to amplify your reach can transform your sourcing strategy. Create engaging content on social media to showcase your products and attract a wider audience. This not only boosts your visibility but can also lead to collaborations with other brands that may offer bulk discounts. Remember to keep an eye on seasonal trends and align your product offerings accordingly; this foresight can help you source items that are in demand, maximizing your profit potential while keeping your investment low.

Lastly, as you embark on your journey of sourcing products on a budget, cultivate a mindset of resilience and motivation. It's essential to stay adaptable and open to new ideas. Experiment with different sourcing methods, learn from your experiences, and don't be afraid to pivot when necessary. Building your empire from home is a marathon, not a sprint, and with persistence, creativity, and the right strategies, you can turn your budget into a powerhouse of opportunity. Keep hustling, and remember that every small step you take brings you closer to your goals!

Creating an Engaging Online Store

Creating an engaging online store is an exciting journey that can open doors to financial freedom and entrepreneurial success, especially for those on a budget. As low-income earners, stay-at-home parents, or aspiring wealth builders, it's crucial to build a digital presence that captivates your audience and keeps them coming back. Start by focusing on user experience; ensure that your online store is visually appealing, easy to navigate, and mobile-friendly. A clean design with high-quality images and concise product descriptions can make a world of difference. Remember, customers are more likely to purchase from a site that feels professional and trustworthy.

Next, harness the power of storytelling to connect with your audience. People love a good story, and sharing your journey can create an emotional bond with your potential customers. Talk about your motivation for starting the business, the challenges you've overcome, and the passion behind your products. This personal touch not only makes your brand more relatable but also encourages customers to support your venture. When they see the heart and soul you've poured into your online store, they're more inclined to become loyal patrons.

Incorporating engaging content is another vital strategy. Consider adding a blog to your online store where you can share valuable insights, tips, and tutorials related to your products. This not only positions you as an expert in your niche but also helps in driving organic traffic to your site. By offering free resources, you can build a community around your brand, encouraging visitors to return for more. Additionally, don't underestimate the power of social media. Use platforms like Instagram and Facebook to showcase your products, share behind-the-scenes glimpses, and interact with your audience. Authentic engagement on social media can significantly boost your online store's visibility.

Utilizing digital marketing strategies is essential for attracting customers to your online store. Start with search engine optimization (SEO) to enhance your site's visibility on search engines. Research relevant keywords that align with your products and incorporate them naturally into your product descriptions and blog posts. Investing time in learning about email marketing can also pay off. Create a mailing list and send out newsletters with exclusive offers, product launches, and engaging content. This not only keeps your customers informed but also helps in building a loyal customer base.

Finally, don't forget to analyze your store's performance and seek feedback from your customers. Use analytics tools to track your website traffic, conversion rates, and customer behavior. Understanding what works and what doesn't will enable you to make data-driven decisions for continuous improvement. Encourage your customers to leave reviews and testimonials; their feedback can provide valuable insights while also serving as social proof to attract new buyers. By embracing these strategies and maintaining a positive, resilient attitude, you can create an online store that not only generates income but also empowers you on your journey as an entrepreneur.

Chapter 7: Achieving Work-Life Balance

Setting Boundaries for Work and Home

Setting boundaries between work and home is crucial for maintaining balance, especially for low-income earners and aspiring entrepreneurs. When you're building your empire from home, it can be easy to let work seep into every corner of your life. This often results in burnout and diminished productivity. To thrive, it's essential to establish clear boundaries that allow you to focus on your hustle while still enjoying precious time with your family and yourself.

Start by defining your work hours. Just like a traditional job, set specific times for when you will work on your projects and stick to them. This creates a routine that not only helps you stay disciplined but also signals to others in your household when you are available and when you need to concentrate. Communicate these hours clearly to your family, so they understand the importance of respecting your work time. When everyone is on the same page, it creates a harmonious environment that fosters productivity and reduces interruptions.

Next, create a dedicated workspace that physically separates your work from your home life. Whether it's a corner of your living room or a separate room, having a designated area for your work can help you mentally switch gears when it's time to focus. Decorate your workspace in a way that inspires you and enhances your motivation. This space should be free of distractions, allowing you to dive into your entrepreneurial pursuits with full concentration, while also making it easier to leave work behind when your scheduled time is over.

Implementing digital boundaries is equally important. With technology at our fingertips, it can be tempting to check emails or respond to messages during family time. Set specific times to check your devices and stick to them. Use apps that allow you to schedule social media posts or emails in advance, freeing up your time for deeper family connections and personal relaxation. This not only helps you to be more present at home but also eliminates the constant pull of work tasks that can disrupt your focus and energy levels.

Finally, practice self-care as a non-negotiable part of your routine. Establishing boundaries is about more than just work and home; it's also about making time for yourself. Engage in activities that recharge your spirit, whether it's exercise, reading, or simply enjoying a quiet moment with a cup of tea. By prioritizing your well-being, you will cultivate resilience and motivation, essential qualities for any aspiring entrepreneur. Remember, building your empire is a marathon, not a sprint. With well-defined boundaries, you'll create a sustainable path to success that honors both your ambitions and your personal life.

Time for Self-Care and Family

In the hustle of building your empire from home, it's easy to forget the importance of self-care and family time. As low-income earners and aspiring entrepreneurs, you may often feel the pressure to maximize every hour, every minute, and every ounce of energy into your side hustles. However, dedicating time for self-care is not just a luxury; it's a crucial investment in your overall well-being and productivity. By nurturing yourself, you become more resilient, motivated, and ultimately, a better entrepreneur. Remember, you can't pour from an empty cup!

Creating a routine that prioritizes self-care doesn't have to be complicated or time-consuming. Start small by dedicating just 15-30 minutes a day to a relaxing activity that brings you joy, whether it's reading a book, practicing yoga, or enjoying a cup of tea in peace. These moments of tranquility can recharge your mind and body, equipping you with the strength to tackle the challenges of building your business. Incorporating these breaks into your day is not only beneficial for your personal health but also allows you to approach your entrepreneurial endeavors with a clearer and more focused mindset.

Equally important is the time spent with your family. As you navigate the demands of entrepreneurship, it's essential to carve out moments to bond with loved ones. Family support can be a powerful motivator on your journey to success. Schedule regular family activities, whether it's game nights, cooking meals together, or simple walks in the park. These experiences create cherished memories and strengthen your support system, reminding you that your entrepreneurial aspirations are not just for you, but for your family as well.

Networking doesn't solely happen in professional settings; it can also flourish within your family circle. Share your entrepreneurial dreams and challenges with family members who can provide encouragement, feedback, or even ideas. Involving your family in your journey can not only help them understand your ambitions but also inspire them to pursue their own goals. By fostering an environment of shared dreams and mutual support, you create a powerful network that can uplift everyone involved.

Finally, remember that balance is key. The journey of building wealth on a budget requires hard work, but it also demands moments of joy and connection. Strive to maintain a healthy work-life balance by setting boundaries for your work hours and staying committed to your self-care and family time. When you prioritize these aspects of life, you cultivate an entrepreneurial mindset that values not just financial success, but holistic well-being. Your business can thrive when you are thriving, so make self-care and family time an integral part of your wealth-building journey.

Strategies to Avoid Burnout

Recognizing the signs of burnout is the first step in avoiding it, especially for those of us juggling multiple responsibilities. If you're a stay-at-home parent or a low-income earner trying to build your empire from home, it's crucial to maintain your energy and enthusiasm. Start by setting clear boundaries between work and personal time. Designate specific hours for your side hustles and stick to them. This will help you create a routine that allows you to recharge, ensuring you don't find yourself overwhelmed and exhausted by the demands of entrepreneurship.

Incorporating short breaks into your work schedule can significantly boost your productivity and morale. Use techniques like the Pomodoro Technique, where you work for 25 minutes and then take a five-minute break. During these breaks, step away from your workspace, stretch, grab a drink, or even take a quick walk. These mini-rejuvenation sessions can help refresh your mind and keep your creative juices flowing, making it easier to return to your tasks with renewed vigor.

Networking with fellow entrepreneurs and side hustlers can provide both support and inspiration, acting as a buffer against burnout. Surrounding yourself with like-minded individuals fosters a sense of community and belonging. Attend local meetups or join online forums to share experiences, tips, and encouragement. Engaging with others will not only keep you motivated but also remind you that you're not alone in your journey, making the challenges seem less daunting.

Prioritizing self-care is essential for maintaining your mental health. Set aside time each week for activities that bring you joy and relaxation, whether that's reading, exercising, or indulging in a hobby. Remember, taking care of yourself is not a luxury; it's a necessity. When you nurture your well-being, you equip yourself to tackle the challenges of building your empire with greater resilience and creativity. This balance will ultimately enhance your productivity and effectiveness as a wealth builder.

Lastly, keeping a positive mindset can be a game changer in avoiding burnout. Focus on your achievements, no matter how small, and celebrate your progress. Develop a gratitude practice by jotting down what you're thankful for each day, which can shift your perspective and keep you motivated. By fostering an entrepreneurial mindset that embraces challenges as opportunities for growth, you'll cultivate the resilience needed to push through tough times without succumbing to burnout. Remember, your journey to wealth is a marathon, not a sprint, and maintaining your passion is key to reaching the finish line.

Chapter 8: Staying Motivated and Resilient

Finding Your 'Why'

Finding your 'Why' is the cornerstone of any successful journey, especially when building your wealth from home. For low-income earners and stay-at-home parents, understanding your motivation can transform the way you approach your financial goals. Your 'Why' is the driving force that ignites your passion and fuels your hustle. It's the reason you wake up each morning ready to chase your dreams, even when the odds seem stacked against you. This sense of purpose can be your most powerful asset, guiding your decisions and keeping you focused on what truly matters.

Identifying your 'Why' begins with introspection. Take a moment to reflect on what you genuinely desire in life. Is it financial freedom, the ability to provide for your family, or perhaps the dream of starting a business that allows you to connect with your community? Write these thoughts down. When you visualize your aspirations, you create a roadmap that leads you toward your goals. Remember, your 'Why' doesn't have to be grand; it simply needs to resonate with you personally. This clarity will help you navigate the challenges ahead and remind you why you're putting in the effort.

Once you've established your 'Why', leverage it to build your entrepreneurial mindset. Your motivation will act as a compass, guiding your actions and decisions. Embrace the hustle muscle by setting small, achievable goals that align with your purpose. This practice not only enhances your confidence but also reinforces your commitment to your vision. Every time you accomplish a goal, however minor, remember to celebrate those wins. They are stepping stones on your journey and reminders of why you started in the first place.

Networking is another vital aspect of your entrepreneurial journey, and your 'Why' can shape your connections. When you articulate your purpose, you attract like-minded individuals who share your vision. Attend local events, join online groups, or participate in social media discussions where you can share your story. Your passion will resonate with others and open doors to collaboration, mentorship, and valuable resources. Building a supportive network can provide you with encouragement and accountability, essential elements when you're trying to balance family commitments and your entrepreneurial aspirations.

Finally, keep your 'Why' at the forefront as you develop resilience and motivation in your journey. There will be setbacks and obstacles, but remembering your purpose can provide the strength to push through. Embrace a growth mindset, viewing challenges as opportunities to learn and grow. Surround yourself with motivational content and engage in skill development that aligns with your goals. The road to wealth-building may be challenging, but with a clear understanding of your 'Why', you'll cultivate the determination and resilience needed to thrive. Your journey is uniquely yours, and the passion that fuels it is the key to creating your empire from home.

Techniques for Staying Motivated

Staying motivated is crucial for anyone looking to build wealth from home, especially for low-income earners and stay-at-home parents juggling multiple responsibilities. One effective technique is to set clear, achievable goals. Break down your long-term vision into smaller, manageable milestones. For instance, if your goal is to launch an e-commerce store, start by setting a timeline for researching products, creating your website, and marketing your brand. Each time you achieve a milestone, celebrate it! This not only boosts your confidence but also reinforces your commitment to your ultimate goal.

Another powerful technique is to establish a daily routine that fosters productivity and aligns with your personal circumstances. As a busy parent or a low-income earner, your time is precious. Carve out specific time blocks each day dedicated solely to your hustle. Whether it's early in the morning or late at night, find those golden hours when you are least distracted. Stick to this routine consistently, and over time, it will become a habit that fuels your motivation and helps you make steady progress toward your entrepreneurial aspirations.

Surrounding yourself with a supportive network is also key to staying motivated. Engage with like-minded individuals who share your entrepreneurial spirit. Join online forums, social media groups, or local meetups focused on entrepreneurial development. Sharing your challenges and successes with others can provide not only emotional support but also practical advice and inspiration. Networking with fellow hustlers can reignite your passion and remind you that you are not alone in your journey to wealth-building.

Incorporating self-care practices into your daily life is essential for maintaining motivation. It is easy to burn out when you're striving for success, especially while managing other responsibilities. Make time for physical activity, meditation, or hobbies that you enjoy. These activities can recharge your mind and body, making you more resilient when facing challenges. Remember, a well-rested and happy individual is far more productive than one who is constantly overwhelmed. Prioritize your well-being, and you will find that motivation flows more naturally.

Finally, embrace a mindset of lifelong learning. The world of entrepreneurship is ever-evolving, and staying curious will keep your motivation alive. Invest time in learning new skills relevant to your side hustles, whether it's digital marketing, e-commerce strategies, or time management techniques. Online courses, podcasts, and books are excellent resources that can provide fresh insights and inspiration. By continuously expanding your knowledge, you not only enhance your capabilities but also cultivate a growth mindset that fuels your drive to succeed.

Building Resilience Through Challenges

Building resilience through challenges is a cornerstone of personal and financial growth, especially for low-income earners and aspiring entrepreneurs. Every setback, whether it's a failed project or a financial hiccup, presents an opportunity to learn and adapt. Embracing these challenges with a positive mindset can transform obstacles into stepping stones toward success. For stay-at-home parents juggling multiple responsibilities, understanding that resilience is built through experience will empower you to tackle each hurdle with confidence and creativity.

As you navigate the world of building your empire from home, remember that challenges are not roadblocks but rather essential elements of your journey. Each experience, good or bad, contributes to your entrepreneurial mindset development. When you encounter difficulties, take a moment to reflect on what went wrong and how you can adjust your approach. This reflection is crucial in developing your "hustle muscle." By pushing through tough times, you not only strengthen your resolve but also gain valuable insights that will serve you well in future endeavors.

Time management techniques become vital as you balance your side hustles with family obligations. Challenges will arise that threaten to derail your carefully laid plans, but with resilience, you can pivot and refocus. Develop a flexible schedule that allows for adjustments when life throws unexpected events your way. Create a daily routine that prioritizes your most important tasks while leaving room for self-care and family time. This balance will help you maintain your energy and enthusiasm, ensuring that you stay motivated even when the going gets tough.

Networking strategies are essential for aspiring entrepreneurs, particularly when facing challenges. Surrounding yourself with a supportive community can make a substantial difference in how you perceive and overcome obstacles. Attend local events, join online groups, and connect with mentors who understand the struggles of building a business from the ground up. Sharing your experiences with others not only fosters collaboration but also builds a safety net of support that can help you bounce back when faced with adversity.

Finally, digital marketing and e-commerce strategies can be daunting, but they are integral to your success as a freelancer or entrepreneur. When challenges arise in these areas, approach them as learning opportunities rather than setbacks. Experiment with different marketing techniques, analyze results, and adjust your strategies accordingly. This iterative process builds your resilience and teaches you to embrace innovation and change. Remember, every successful entrepreneur has faced their share of challenges; it's the ability to rise, adapt, and thrive that ultimately leads to success in building your empire from home.

Chapter 9: Developing Your Skills

Identifying Marketable Skills

Identifying marketable skills is a crucial stepping stone for anyone looking to create a thriving enterprise from the comfort of home. In today's fast-paced digital economy, the opportunities are plentiful, but it's essential to know which skills can translate into income. Start by evaluating your current abilities and experiences. Whether you are a stay-at-home parent managing a household or a low-income earner seeking extra income, everyone has something valuable to offer. Take stock of what you do well, whether it's organizing events, crafting engaging social media posts, or providing customer service. Each of these skills can be the foundation on which to build your entrepreneurial journey.

Next, consider the skills that are in high demand in the marketplace. Research current trends in your niche, such as digital marketing, e-commerce, and freelance services. Platforms like Google Trends, LinkedIn, and various freelance websites can provide insights into what employers and clients are seeking. Skills like SEO, content creation, social media management, and basic graphic design can open doors to various side hustles. By aligning your existing skills with market demand, you position yourself as a competitive candidate, ready to seize opportunities as they arise.

Networking plays a pivotal role in skill identification and enhancement. Connect with like-minded individuals who are also on their journey toward financial independence. Attend local meetups, join online forums, or participate in social media groups focused on entrepreneurship. These connections can lead to valuable insights about which skills are currently sought after and how to develop them. Furthermore, sharing your aspirations and skills with others can spark collaborations, mentorships, and even job opportunities that you might not have found on your own.

Once you identify your marketable skills, it's time to invest in developing and refining them. Online courses, webinars, and workshops are excellent resources for skill enhancement. Many platforms offer free or low-cost options tailored to busy schedules, making it easier for stay-at-home parents or those with limited time to learn and grow. Dedicating even a small amount of time each week to skill development can yield significant returns. As you build your expertise, you'll gain confidence, allowing you to tackle larger projects or explore new avenues in your entrepreneurial journey.

Remember, the path to building wealth is not solely about financial investments; it's also about investing in yourself. Identifying and honing your marketable skills can set the stage for a successful side hustle or full-fledged business. With determination, creativity, and the right mindset, you can transform your abilities into a sustainable source of income. Embrace the process, stay motivated, and watch as your skills become the cornerstone of your financial empire.

Free and Low-Cost Learning Resources

In today's digital age, the opportunities for learning and self-improvement have never been more accessible, especially for those looking to build wealth on a budget. Free and low-cost learning resources abound, offering invaluable knowledge and skills that can propel you toward your goals. Whether you're a stay-at-home parent looking to start a side hustle, a low-income earner striving for financial freedom, or an aspiring entrepreneur eager to sharpen your skills, there is a wealth of information at your fingertips. Embrace this chance to learn and grow without the burden of hefty tuition fees!

Online platforms such as Coursera, edX, and Khan Academy provide a treasure trove of courses covering everything from digital marketing to time management techniques. Many of these courses are offered for free or at a minimal cost, making it easy for you to gain expertise from industry professionals. As you dive into these resources, you'll find that building your hustle muscle is not just about working hard; it's about working smart, and these courses can equip you with the strategies you need to maximize your efforts.

Podcasts and webinars have surged in popularity, offering insights from successful entrepreneurs and experts in various fields. Platforms like Spotify and Apple Podcasts host countless shows focused on entrepreneurial mindset development, motivation, and resilience. Tuning into these discussions can provide you with fresh perspectives and practical tips that you can apply to your journey. The best part? You can listen while managing your household or during your daily commutes, making it easy to integrate learning into your busy schedule.

Networking does not have to be an expensive endeavor. Social media platforms such as LinkedIn and Facebook groups can connect you with like-minded individuals who share your entrepreneurial aspirations. Engaging in online communities allows you to exchange ideas, seek advice, and form connections that could lead to collaborative opportunities. Additionally, many local libraries and community centers offer free workshops and networking events that can further expand your circle and provide support as you embark on your entrepreneurial journey.

Finally, don't overlook the power of books and e-books, which are often available at a fraction of the cost of traditional courses. Libraries offer a vast selection of resources on e-commerce strategies for beginners, skill development for freelancers, and work-life balance techniques tailored for hustlers. Many authors also share their expertise through free resources or affordable e-books. By investing time into consuming these materials, you'll not only enhance your knowledge but also inspire your journey toward financial empowerment. The path to building your empire from home is filled with opportunities—seize them with enthusiasm and determination!

Turning Skills into Income Streams

In today's fast-paced world, the ability to transform your skills into income streams is not just a dream; it's an achievable reality. Whether you're a stay-at-home parent, a low-income earner, or someone eager to build wealth on a budget, harnessing your unique talents can open the door to financial freedom. Embrace your skills, whether they are crafting, writing, coding, or digital marketing, and remember that every ability you possess has the potential to generate income. The key is to identify what you love to do and how it can serve others while bringing in cash.

To kickstart your journey, begin by assessing your current skills and interests. Make a list of everything you excel at or enjoy doing. Are you great at graphic design? Perhaps you have a knack for social media management? By pinpointing your strengths, you can strategically choose a side hustle that not only aligns with your passions but also fills a gap in the market. This alignment will keep you motivated and engaged as you work toward turning your skills into a lucrative venture.

Once you've identified your skill set, it's time to dive into the entrepreneurial mindset. Cultivating this mindset involves being proactive, embracing challenges, and viewing setbacks as opportunities for growth. Surround yourself with like-minded individuals who inspire and motivate you. Networking is essential; connect with fellow entrepreneurs, attend local meetups, or join online communities. These connections can lead to invaluable advice and potential collaborations that can elevate your side hustle to the next level.

Time management is another crucial aspect for those balancing multiple responsibilities. As a busy parent or a full-time worker, finding time to invest in your side hustle can be challenging. Implement effective time management techniques, such as setting specific goals, prioritizing tasks, and creating a dedicated workspace. Block out time in your schedule where you can focus solely on your project, ensuring that you make steady progress without feeling overwhelmed. Remember, every small step forward is a step toward financial independence.

Finally, never underestimate the power of digital marketing in building your income streams. With the right strategies, you can reach a vast audience without breaking the bank. Learn the basics of social media marketing, content creation, and e-commerce strategies to promote your services or products effectively. Harness platforms like Etsy, Fiverr, or social media to showcase your skills and attract clients. Stay resilient and motivated, even when faced with challenges; remember, every successful entrepreneur started somewhere, and with perseverance, you too can turn your skills into a thriving income stream.

Chapter 10: Your Path to Wealth

Creating a Sustainable Financial Plan

Creating a sustainable financial plan is the cornerstone of building your empire from home. For low-income earners and stay-at-home parents, the prospect of financial stability can feel daunting, but it is entirely achievable with a strategic approach. Start by assessing your current financial situation. Gather all your income sources, including side hustles, and list your expenses. This comprehensive view allows you to identify where your money is going and understand your financial landscape. With this knowledge, you can set realistic short-term and long-term financial goals that align with your dreams of entrepreneurship and wealth-building.

Once you have a clear picture of your finances, it's time to create a budget that reflects your goals. Embrace the concept of "living below your means." This doesn't mean depriving yourself but rather prioritizing your spending. Allocate funds toward essentials and savings while carving out a portion for investments in your side hustle or entrepreneurial endeavors. Remember, every dollar saved is a step closer to financial freedom. Utilize budgeting tools or apps to track your expenses and make adjustments as needed, ensuring that your plan remains flexible yet structured.

Investing in your personal and professional development is crucial for building a sustainable financial future. Consider online courses that enhance your skills in digital marketing, e-commerce, or any niche that ignites your passion. These investments can lead to higher earning potential and greater job satisfaction. Additionally, seek out networking opportunities, both online and offline, to connect with like-minded individuals who share your entrepreneurial spirit. Building relationships can open doors to collaborations, mentorships, and new income streams that can significantly boost your financial plan.

Time management plays a pivotal role in executing your financial plan effectively. As a stay-at-home parent or a side hustler, finding the balance between work and family can be challenging. Create a schedule that allocates specific time slots for your entrepreneurial activities, ensuring that you stay focused and productive. Set achievable milestones and celebrate your progress, no matter how small. This will not only keep you motivated but also help you maintain a work-life balance that allows you to thrive in both your personal and professional life.

Lastly, resilience and motivation are key factors in sustaining your financial plan. There will be challenges along the way, but embracing a growth mindset can turn obstacles into opportunities. Surround yourself with supportive individuals who encourage your journey, and remember to practice self-care to maintain your mental well-being. Celebrate your achievements, and don't hesitate to reassess and adjust your plan as needed. With determination and a clear financial strategy, you can create a sustainable financial plan that empowers you to build wealth and achieve your dreams from the comfort of your home.

Tracking Your Progress

Tracking your progress is an essential element in the journey of building wealth on a budget. For low-income earners, stay-at-home parents, and aspiring entrepreneurs, keeping an eye on your advancements not only boosts motivation but also helps you make informed decisions as you navigate through your financial landscape. Each small victory, whether it's completing a course or hitting a sales milestone in your side hustle, deserves recognition. When you track these wins, you create a roadmap that showcases your growth, reinforcing your entrepreneurial mindset and fueling your ambition.

One of the most effective ways to track progress is through goal setting. Establish clear, achievable goals that align with your overall vision of wealth-building. Break these down into smaller, actionable steps and set deadlines for each. Whether you aim to increase your e-commerce sales by a certain percentage or learn a new skill that enhances your freelance offerings, having specific targets keeps you focused and accountable. Celebrate each milestone you reach, no matter how small, because these celebrations build your hustle muscle and provide the encouragement needed to tackle the next challenge.

Incorporating time management techniques is crucial for those balancing multiple responsibilities. Use tools like planners, apps, or spreadsheets to monitor your daily and weekly tasks. Allocate time blocks dedicated to your side hustle, skill development, and networking efforts. Regularly reviewing how you spend your time allows you to identify areas for improvement and ensures that you are making the most of your limited hours. As a stay-at-home parent or someone with a full-time job, effective time management can transform your productivity and lead to significant progress in your entrepreneurial endeavors.

Networking is another vital component of tracking your progress. Connect with other like-minded individuals who share your aspirations. Join online forums, attend local meetups, or participate in social media groups focused on entrepreneurship. By engaging with others, you can share your successes, gather feedback, and receive support when needed. These interactions not only provide valuable insights but also help you measure your growth against others, motivating you to push further and strive for excellence.

Lastly, don't forget the importance of resilience and motivation in your journey to wealth. Reflect on your experiences regularly, noting both successes and setbacks. This practice helps you understand your personal growth trajectory and inspires you to keep moving forward despite obstacles. Embrace challenges as learning opportunities; they are part of the entrepreneurial process. By diligently tracking your progress, you maintain a clear vision of your goals and the steps necessary to achieve them, ultimately building the empire you desire from the comfort of your home.

Celebrating Your Wins and Planning for More

Celebrating your wins, no matter how small, is a crucial part of building your wealth and maintaining your motivation. Every step forward, from landing your first freelance gig to making your first sale in your e-commerce store, deserves recognition. Take a moment to reflect on these achievements. Write them down in a dedicated journal or share them with your accountability partner or family. This practice not only boosts your confidence but also reinforces the belief that you are capable of achieving greater things. Remember, each win adds a brick to your empire, and acknowledging them keeps the momentum alive and kicking.

Once you've taken the time to celebrate, it's essential to channel that positive energy into planning for your next milestones. Set specific, achievable goals that align with your vision of wealth. Whether it's increasing your side hustle income by a particular percentage, expanding your skills through online courses, or networking with five new contacts this month, having clear objectives helps you stay focused. Break these goals down into manageable tasks so you can tackle them bit by bit. This strategy not only makes large projects seem less daunting but also provides you with a roadmap to success.

Networking is a powerful tool for aspiring entrepreneurs, especially for those building their empire from home. Celebrate your wins by sharing your journey and connecting with others who can inspire you. Attend local meet-ups, join online forums, or participate in social media groups relevant to your niche. Each interaction can lead to valuable insights, collaborations, or even new opportunities. Remember, your network is your net worth. The more you engage with like-minded individuals, the more you'll find potential partners, mentors, and supporters who can help propel your journey forward.

As you plan for future successes, don't forget to balance the hustle with self-care. It's easy to get caught up in the grind, especially as a stay-at-home parent or low-income earner striving to build wealth. Schedule time for yourself and your loved ones to recharge your energy. Engaging in hobbies, exercise, or simply enjoying family time can rejuvenate your mind and improve your productivity. A well-balanced life fuels creativity and resilience, enabling you to face challenges head-on while keeping your entrepreneurial spirit alive.

Finally, stay motivated by continuously learning and adapting. The entrepreneurial landscape is ever-changing, especially in the digital age. Invest time in skill development relevant to your goals. Whether it's mastering digital marketing strategies or understanding e-commerce platforms, every piece of knowledge you gain will equip you for your next big win. Celebrate your growth along the way, and remember that perseverance is key. Each challenge you overcome fortifies your hustle muscle, making you a stronger, more resilient entrepreneur ready to tackle whatever comes next.

www.ingramcontent.com/pod-product-compliance
Lightning Source LLC
Chambersburg PA
CBHW070359230526
45471CB00006B/2642